THINK BIG

THE GREATEST IDEAS IN ENTERTAINMENT

IZZI HOWELL

Cavendish Square

Published in 2026 by Cavendish Square Publishing, LLC
2544 Clinton Street, Buffalo, NY 14224

First published in Great Britain in 2022 by Wayland

Website: cavendishsq.com

Author and editor: Izzi Howell
Designer: Clare Nicholas

The publisher would like to thank the following for permission to reproduce their pictures:
Alamy: Everett Collection Inc 7t, Granger Historical Picture Archive 7b, REUTERS 25b; Julian Baker: 6br and 10t; Getty: Alfred Eisenstaedt/The LIFE Picture Collection 6l, Kirn Vintage Stock/Corbis 8t, Yvonne Hemsey 8b, Earl Theisen 12b, Dale de la Rey/ Bloomberg 13t, Jeff Gritchen/MediaNews Group/Orange County Register 15b, Dick Lewis/NY Daily News Archive 16, François DUCASSE/Gamma-Rapho 17b, The Asahi Shimbun 19b, Dave Hogan 20b, Allen J. Schaben/Los Angeles Times 29b; Julian Baker 6br and 10t; Dr Lidia Galdino 22; Shutterstock: bez_bretelky cover top, Mark Nazh cover bottom, Everett Collection 4, Roman Samborskyi 5l, Vladimir Yazev 5r, vvoe 9t, natatravel 9b, Supakorn Limteerayos 10b, EQRoy 11t, zaidi razak 11b, Roberto Galan 12t, V_E 13cl, ChameleonsEye 13cr, Jesseniasarah9 13b, Stefano Buttafoco 14t, Dfree 14b, Sebastian Barros 15t, Axel Bueckert 17t, robtek 18t and 18b, Wachiwit 19t and 31, EcoPrint 20t, BMCL 21t, Prometheus72 21b, Song_about_summer 23, Rawpixel.com 24, Twin Design 25t, testing 26, VVproduct 27t, Matthew Corley 27b, ESB Professional 28, ESB Professional 29t.

All design elements from Shutterstock.

Cataloging-in-Publication Data

Names: Howell, Izzi.
Title: The greatest ideas in entertainment / Izzi Howell.
Description: Buffalo, New York : Cavendish Square Publishing, 2026. |
Series: Think big | Includes index, glossary, and bibliographic information
Identifiers: ISBN 9781502675309 (pbk) | ISBN 9781502675316 (library bound) |
ISBN 9781502675323 (ebook)
Subjects: LCSH: Amusement parks—Juvenile Literature | Cinematography—Juvenile Literature |
Entertainment events—Juvenile Literature | LEGO toys—Juvenile Literature |
Star Wars films—Juvenile Literature | Video games--Juvenile Literature |
Word games—Juvenile Literature
Classification: LCC GT2480 H69 2026 | DDC 790.1 --dc25

CPSIA compliance information: Batch #CS26CSQ: For further information contact Cavendish Square Publishing LLC at 1-877-980-4450.

Printed in the United States of America

Contents

People have always found ways to have fun, but the 20th and 21st centuries saw many pioneering developments in entertainment. New technology and ideas resulted in groundbreaking new forms of entertainment.

Where Do We Begin?

For much of human history, people worked very hard and had little free time in which they could relax and have fun. After the Industrial Revolution (c.1760–1900), during which we began to use machines to do work for us, people had more time to enjoy themselves. In addition, new laws reducing the number of work hours a week meant more time for leisure.

Thinking Big

The 20th century was a time of huge technological changes. We were introduced to many inventions that we now take for granted, such as the TV, phone, and computers. These technological developments also had an impact on entertainment and resulted in new machines that were great fun, such as gaming consoles.

Chess has been a popular form of entertainment since the 6th century CE.

The smartphone is one of the most important recent developments in entertainment. It combines many different forms of entertainment that used to exist separately, including games, TV shows, books, and music.

THINK BIG!

Research some popular forms of entertainment from the past, such as card games or a hoop and a stick. Reinvent one of these forms of entertainment for the 21st century market. How could you use the latest developments in technology to add new features?

GENIUS

James Cameron (1954–) is a Canadian film producer who is responsible for some of the biggest ever hit films. His 1997 film *Titanic* became the highest grossing film of all time until Cameron beat his own record with the release of *Avatar* in 2009. *Avatar* was one of the most successful 3D films and led to many companies launching 3D TVs.

Technicolor

The Big Idea

The colors in early color films were painted on by hand! This was followed by the first Technicolor films, which used two strips of film with red and green filters to make a range of different colors. In 1932, Technicolor realized that they could make even more colors by adding a third blue strip of film. This made the colors in their films much more realistic.

We often use the word "technicolor" to describe something very brightly colored, but did you know that this word comes from the American company who created some of the first types of color film? The Technicolor three-strip camera, launched in 1932, was the beginning of realistic color films as we know them today.

Technicolor three-strip cameras were very large because extra space was needed inside for the red, green, and blue strips.

How Did It Work?

Inside a Technicolor three-strip camera was a prism that split light into three parts. One third of the light passed through a green filter. The image recorded from this light only had green tones. The other two parts passed through a magenta (red + blue) filter and recorded film with red and blue tones. After processing, the three strips were brought together to create one colorful film. A black and white layer was added for sharpness.

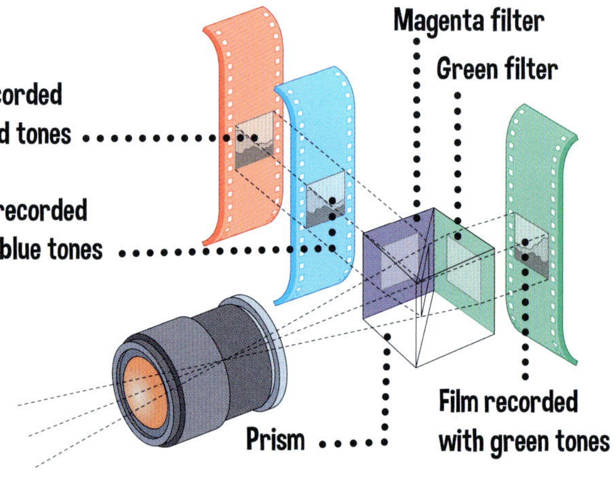

Where Did It Lead?

The bright, exciting colors of Technicolor films such as *Snow White and the Seven Dwarfs* (1937), *The Wizard of Oz* (1939) and *Gone with the Wind* (1939) helped to make them hugely successful. Many of these early films still appear vibrant, even to modern audiences. Studios continued to use Technicolor three-strip film until the 1950s, when other, cheaper color film processes became more popular.

GENIUS

Natalie Kalmus (1882–1965) co-founded Technicolor with her husband Herbert Kalmus. She worked as the on-site Technicolor color director for over 300 films, helping the costume and scenery departments to make sure everything would look its best on Technicolor film. Her knowledge and expertise led to the beautiful, colorful Technicolor films we know today.

The wide range of colors available in Technicolor influenced films. For example, the ruby slippers in *The Wizard of Oz* were originally silver. They were changed to red to show off the contrast against the yellow brick road that could be achieved by filming in Technicolor.

THINK BIG!

Research the science behind red, green, and blue color mixing. What other devices use this system? Which systems use CMYK instead?

Scrabble

Scrabble is one of the best-known board games around the world. The idea behind the game is very simple. Players win points by making words from letter tiles.

The Big Idea

The creator of Scrabble, Alfred Butts, wanted to invent a new board game. He saw a gap in the market for a word game where players received scores. He came up with an idea that combined anagrams and crossword puzzles. Butts worked with an entrepreneur called James Brunot to release the final version of the game, which they called Scrabble, in 1948.

A family playing Scrabble in the 1950s, a few years after its release.

GENIUS

American Alfred Butts (1899–1993) was originally an architect, but he lost his job in the Great Depression in the 1930s. He decided to invent a board game to make extra money, and so Scrabble was born!

What Happened?

Scrabble slowly became popular and sales took a great leap when a large American department store started selling the game. Ever since, it has been a well-loved board game. Today, it is found in three out of five U.S. homes and versions of the game are available in more than 30 languages.

The Russian edition of Scrabble features the Cyrillic alphabet.

Where Did It Lead?

Scrabble inspired many other word board games, such as Boggle and Bananagrams, as well as online word games such as Words with Friends. You can also play Scrabble online via Facebook. Top Scrabble players from around the world challenge each other in tournaments.

Boggle was first released in 1972. Players look for adjacent letters in the 16 dice that form words.

THINK BIG!

Use Alfred Butts' approach of combining two types of game to design a new game. It could be a word game, a number game, or a strategy game. Try it out on your family and friends.

LEGO

LEGO is a type of plastic construction toy, mainly consisting of plastic bricks. The first LEGO sets were very simple, but the brand has grown over time to include huge, complex models, working robots, and many themed sets.

The Big Idea

The LEGO Group originally made wooden objects and toys. In 1949, they launched their first plastic bricks, thanks to new technology that allowed them to mold the tiny shapes. However, these early plastic bricks didn't all fit together. It wasn't until 1958 that the modern interlocking LEGO brick was created, and the endless possibilities of LEGO began.

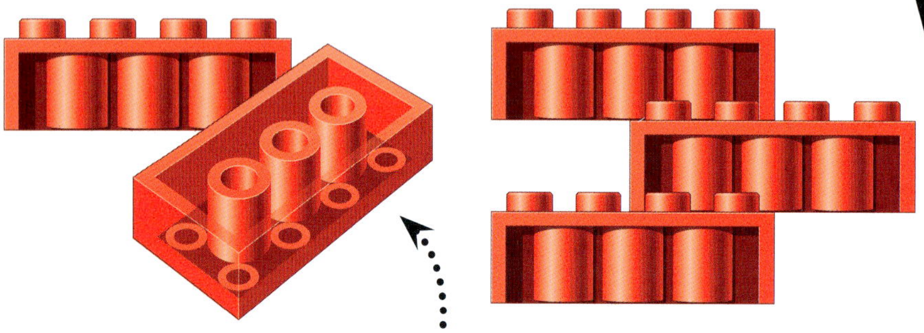

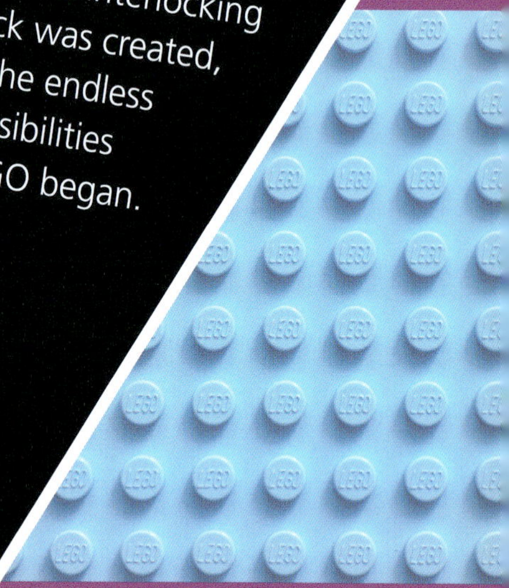

The interlocking structure of the LEGO bricks means that they are very sturdy when assembled, but also easy to take apart.

How Did It Work?

Interlocking LEGO bricks provided a system for creative play with limitless options for building and recreating. At first, the sets were made up of simple pieces that could be combined in different ways. Over time, special pieces such as minifigures and wheels provided new opportunities to create.

This house is built out of basic LEGO pieces along with special parts such as doors, windows, and fences.

Miniature LEGO landmarks and villages are built in Legoland theme parks, such as this model of the Forbidden City in Beijing, in Legoland Malaysia.

Star Wars LEGO contains minifigures of important characters, such as Darth Vader.

Where Did It Lead?

The first Legoland theme park opened in Denmark in 1968. There are now many other Legolands around the world. Video games, board games, and films based on LEGO sets and characters have been released, with great success. LEGO has also released special sets based on films, including the *Harry Potter* and *Star Wars* series.

GENIUS

Ole Kirk Kristiansen (1891–1958) was a Danish carpenter and founder of the LEGO Group. He overcame many setbacks in his working life, including economic problems in Denmark, world wars, and the loss of his factory in a fire. Kristiansen always made it his priority to only produce top-quality work. This is one of the reasons for LEGO's lasting appeal.

THINK BIG!

Set yourself a LEGO building challenge. Choose 40 blocks and try to build as many different objects or structures as possible. If you don't have any LEGO at home, see if you can borrow some from a friend.

Disneyland

Disneyland is a huge amusement park near Los Angeles, California. It is based on the films of Walt Disney and was designed and built with his supervision. Disneyland was one of the first theme parks, inspiring many others to create fun amusement parks around the world.

The Big Idea

Amusement parks with simple rides, food stalls, and attractions first became popular in the early 1900s. In the 1940s, Walt Disney was inspired to create an amusement park based on his animated films and cartoons. Disneyland, which opened in 1955, was the first amusement park based around one theme, or theme park.

How Did It Work?

Disneyland had many different attractions, designed to offer something for everyone: roller coasters, boat trips, live entertainment, food and drink, firework shows, parades, and scenes from films. It had a ready-made fan base, as people already loved Disney films and cartoons.

Some staff at Disneyland dress up and act like characters from Disney films, such as Snow White.

Walt Disney (far left) and his team study a model for Disneyland.

GENIUS

Walt Disney (1901–1966) was an American animator, writer, and founder of The Walt Disney Company. He was a cartoon pioneer, creating some of the most iconic cartoon characters, including Mickey Mouse and Donald Duck. During his lifetime, he expanded The Walt Disney Company with projects such as Disneyland.

Where Did It Lead?

Disneyland has adapted to keep up with new films released by Disney. Other Disney theme parks have also opened across the USA and in other countries, such as France, Japan, and China. Other companies have since established theme parks based on their products.

The Flash ride at Disneyland Hong Kong takes riders 72 feet (22 m) into the air and spins them around at speeds of up to 37 mph (60 kph)!

Other famous theme parks

Universal Studios in California, USA, based on Universal films and TV shows (opened 1964)

Warner Bros. Movie World in Australia, based on Warner Bros. films and TV shows (opened 1991)

Parc Astérix in France, based on the *Asterix* comic books (opened 1989)

THINK BIG!

Design a theme park based on one of your interests. It could be a film, a book, a TV show, or something else. Decide which attractions it will have and draw a map to show its different features.

Star Wars

From the release of the first film in 1977, *Star Wars* has become a global phenomenon. The intergalactic universe from the films has been developed into a massive brand, including films, books, TV shows, merchandise, and much more.

The Big Idea

The events of *Star Wars* take place in "a galaxy far, far away," where humans, aliens, and robots can easily travel from planet to planet. Good and evil characters fight each other, often using a mysterious power called "the Force."

Darth Vader is the iconic villain of the original *Star Wars* trilogy.

GENIUS

George Lucas (1944–) is the American creator of the *Star Wars* franchise. He wrote and directed many of the earlier films, which were created by his production company Lucasfilm. He is one of the most successful filmmakers of all time, thanks to *Star Wars* and his other popular films, such as the *Indiana Jones* franchise.

How Did It Happen?

After the first *Star Wars* film was a box-office hit, George Lucas was able to expand his original story into two further films in 1980 and 1983. The runaway success of this trilogy led to a trilogy of prequels to the original films released between 1999 and 2005, and a trilogy of sequels between 2015 and 2019. The gaps between trilogies have created a fan base of many different ages, as new films were released during the childhoods of different generations.

These young *Star Wars* fans in Colombia are dressed up as different characters from *Star Wars* films and TV shows. *Star Wars* fans often attend events in costume.

Where Did It Lead?

In 2012, George Lucas sold his production company Lucasfilm to Disney for over 4 billion dollars. This meant that he no longer had the rights to produce anything related to the *Star Wars* universe. Disney has greatly expanded the *Star Wars* franchise, producing the latest trilogy of films, several spin-off TV and film projects, and launching new *Star Wars* areas at their theme parks.

THINK BIG!

Spin-offs, such as additional films, TV shows, and books, have been key to the success of the *Star Wars* brand. Choose a film that you enjoy and design one or more spin-offs to go with it. It could be a sequel or a prequel to the film, a TV show, merchandise, games, or something even more unusual!

In the *Star Wars* area in Disneyland, California, there are several rides (such as the Millennium Falcon ride shown here), shops to purchase merchandise, and even restaurants that serve unusual foods from the films, such as blue milk!

Sony Walkman

The Sony Walkman was the first affordable personal stereo. It allowed people to listen to music on the move.

The Big Idea

Before the release of the Walkman in 1979, people only had portable radios. They couldn't listen to their own music outside the home. This changed forever with the arrival of the Walkman. The first Walkmans had tape cassette players, which was one of the main ways of listening to music at that time.

People listening to their Walkmans on the New York City Subway in 1981.

Sony sold over 200 million Walkmans from 1979 to 2010, when they were officially discontinued.

How Did It Work?

Cassette technology had been around since 1963, but no one had thought to take advantage of its small, portable size until Sony developed the Walkman. It was powered with just two AA batteries, which kept it small and light. The Walkman's headphones made it particularly popular with young people who wanted their music to be private.

GENIUS

Akio Morita (1921–1999) was the Japanese co-founder and chairman of Sony – the global electronics company that produced the Walkman. Morita was keen to develop a portable music player, although other people at Sony had doubts. It went on to become one of Sony's most popular products in the 1980s and '90s.

Where Did It Lead?

The product became so widespread that the name Walkman became a general term for any personal stereo, even those from other brands. When CDs took over from cassettes, the Walkman was reissued as a portable CD player – the CD Walkman. Later, people moved on to listen to music on MP3 players, such as the iPod, and then smartphones.

THINK BIG!

Design a portable version of another household appliance. How can you reduce its size while still keeping its features? Think about power supply and how to carry it.

NES

The NES (Nintendo Entertainment System) was one of the first game consoles to make its way into homes around the world. Many games that are still hugely popular today began on the NES.

The Big Idea

Nintendo's NES console was first launched in Japan in 1983 as the Famicom. At this time, the video games industry was crashing in the USA because there were too many different consoles and low-quality games on the market. People were switching over to computer games instead. However, Nintendo showed the world that the NES was different and it became a huge hit when it reached the USA.

Nintendo released new games for the NES, such as Super Mario Bros., as well as arcade games that were already popular, such as Donkey Kong.

The NES was made up of the control deck and detachable controllers. Games were loaded on cartridges.

How was it different?

The NES had 8-bit graphics, which made its gameplay look much better than previous games. All of the games released by Nintendo or external developers for the NES were checked and tested to make sure they reached a high standard. The NES also didn't look like a toy, which helped customers take it more seriously.

Control deck

Game cartridge

Controller

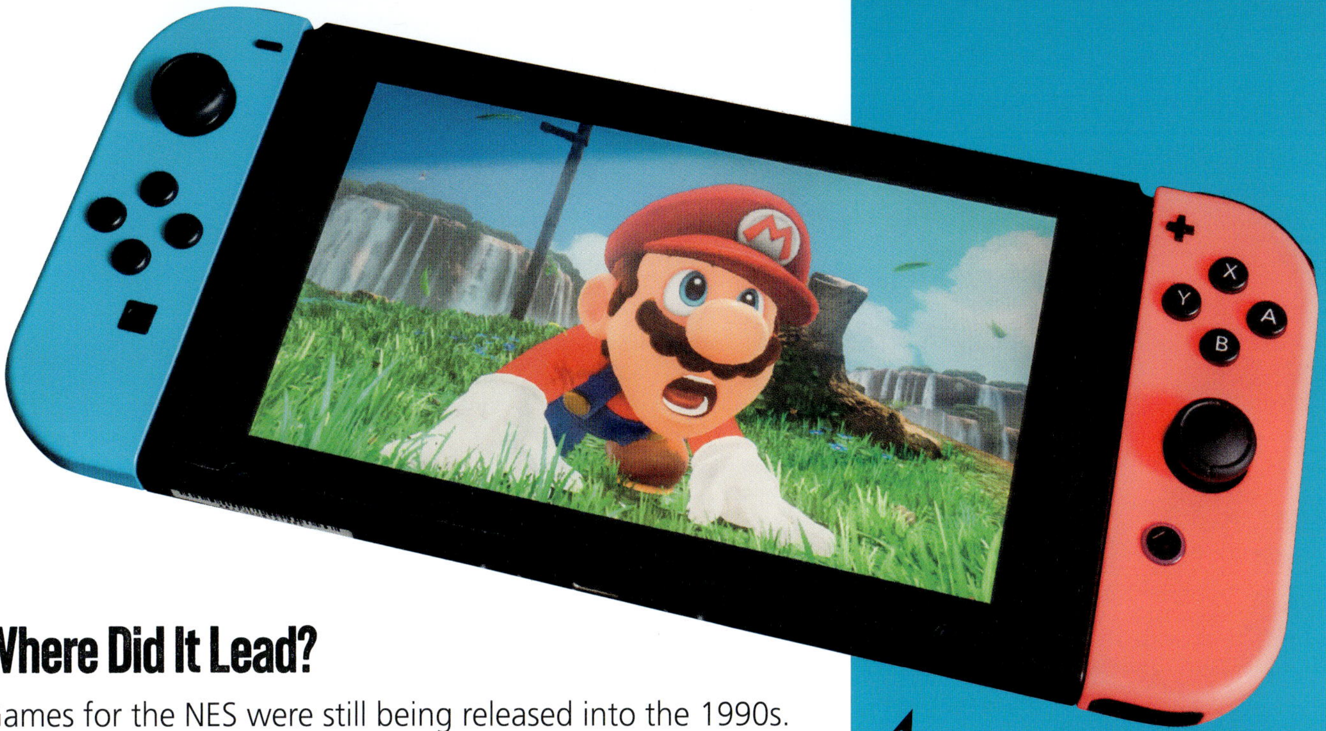

Where Did It Lead?

Games for the NES were still being released into the 1990s. It is estimated that 60 million NESs were sold overall. The popularity of the NES proved that video games weren't just a trend. It helped to revive the video game market, which continues to be very strong today. The NES also launched a number of incredibly popular games series, including The Legend of Zelda and Final Fantasy.

Some of the original NES game series, such as Super Mario, were released on subsequent Nintendo consoles, including the Nintendo Switch.

GENIUS

Hiroshi Yamauchi (1927–2013) was president of Nintendo from 1949 to 2002. He totally reinvented the Japanese company, turning it from being a playing-card manufacturer to a global billion-dollar video-game company.

THINK BIG!

Design your own video game. Think about the characters, the setting, and the gameplay. Draw scenes from the game to present your ideas.

Live Aid

Live Aid was a series of charity concerts held on July 13, 1985. Many huge names in music came together to raise money to help stop famine in Ethiopia.

The Big Idea

In 1983, Ethiopia was hit by a terrible famine due to drought and political problems. In 1984, British musicians Bob Geldof and Midge Ure were inspired to record a Christmas song to raise money to help people affected by the famine. Their single "Do They Know It's Christmas?" featured well-known singers and bands, and sold over three million copies.

How Did It Work?

After the success of the single, Geldof and Ure came up with the idea for a fundraising event called Live Aid. Two huge Live Aid concerts took place in London and Philadelphia, while many other smaller events happened around the world. Over 75 of the biggest names in music at the time, including Queen, U2, David Bowie, Elton John, and Madonna, performed at the concerts. Around 1.5 billion viewers worldwide watched the concerts on TV.

Over 70,000 people attended the Live Aid concert at Wembley Stadium in London.

The Live 8 concerts took place in London (shown here), USA, Canada, and Germany.

Where Did It Lead?

During the concerts, viewers were encouraged to call in and donate money. They raised $127 million, which went to support people affected by the famine. Publicity from the concert encouraged more countries to send aid to Ethiopia. In 2005, Bob Geldof followed up on the Live Aid concerts with the Live 8 events, which raised awareness of global poverty.

GENIUS

Bob Geldof (1951–) is an Irish singer and political activist. He became famous in the late 1970s as the lead singer of the Boomtown Rats, but today he is best known as the organizer of Live Aid and the co-founder of Band Aid. In 1986, he received an honorary knighthood for his charity work.

THINK BIG!

Choose a good cause or charity and come up with a campaign to raise money for it. You could make something or offer your services to others.

File Streaming

Streaming allows people to receive audio and visual files from the internet as a continuous flow. Streaming music and video is an easy way to enjoy a huge range of content whenever you want, wherever you want.

The Big Idea

Up until the 2000s, very few people had a good enough home internet connection to stream content. The lack of bandwidth made the files stop and start frequently. The arrival of broadband internet, along with an increase in the number of people with internet access, finally made streaming a possibility.

GENIUS

Dr. Lidia Galdino is a Brazilian electrical engineer and researcher. In 2020, she set the world record for top internet speed, creating a connection in her laboratory that works three million times faster than the standard home internet. Her connection is so fast that it could download 15,000 films in one second! These types of breakthroughs will help us to get faster home broadband in the future.

How Does It Work?

When you click play on an audio or music file, it sends a signal to a web server. The web server begins to constantly send back small amounts of data that allow you to start watching or listening immediately. You never hold a copy of the file on your device, which makes it very hard to illegally download or share it.

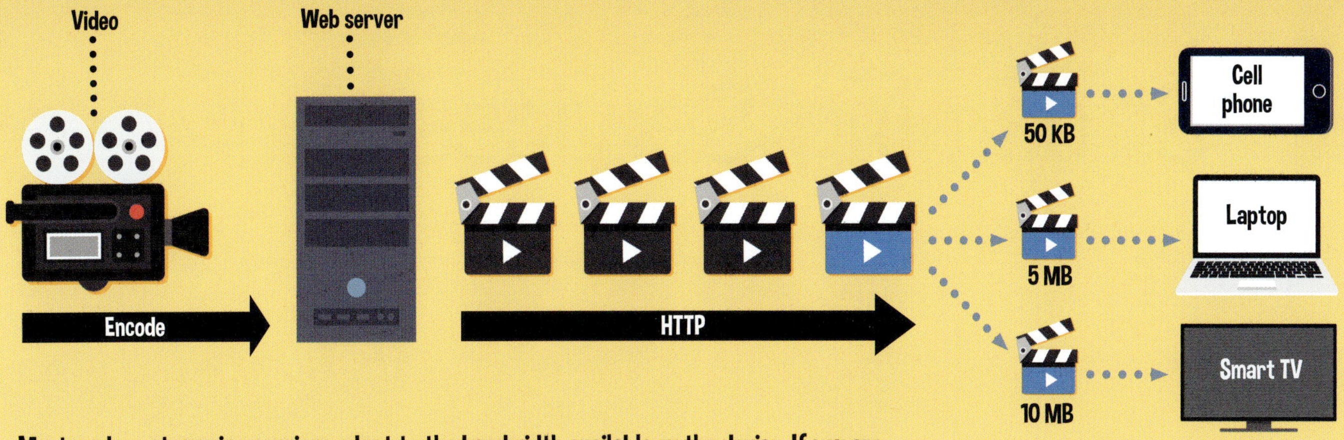

Most modern streaming services adapt to the bandwidth available on the device. If you are streaming a file on a phone with mobile internet connection, the quality of the stream will be lower than on a computer connected to WiFi, for example.

Where Did It Lead?

Many companies launched streaming services (see pages 24–25) once they saw that more people would be able to stream content at home. As well as pre-recorded songs and videos, many services also offer live streaming services. These allow people to watch live events such as concerts, sporting events, and conferences, wherever they are. In 2024, *Taylor Swift: The Eras Tour* was the most streamed music movie ever on Disney +! The concert had only been performed in some cities. Thanks to streaming, many people around the world were able to see it for the first time.

Live streamed concerts often offer a much better view of the stage than attending in person!

THINK BIG!

Research the differences between dial-up and broadband internet connections. Think about speed, the way in which we access the internet, and price. How has our use of the internet changed as a result? Predict how the internet will have changed again 20 years from now.

Streaming Services

Streaming services offer access to a huge range of audio and video files. Today, they are mostly available as freemium or paid subscriptions, which solves the legal problems connected to file sharing.

The Big Idea

Attitudes toward music changed forever with the launch of the Napster online file-sharing service in 1999. Napster allowed people to upload MP3 files from their computer, share them with others and download new songs for free. Suddenly, people could have access to practically any song in the world, rather than being restricted to the CDs, tapes, or vinyl records in their music collection.

What Happened?

However, Napster quickly attracted the attention of record companies who were losing huge amounts of money. As many people were sharing one music file, record companies weren't receiving payment from each consumer any more. Many record companies and some individual artists, including Metallica and Dr. Dre, sued Napster, and it was forced to shut down in 2001. However, people still wanted easy access to music beyond their own personal collection, as well as the option to watch TV shows and films on demand.

While the Walkman (see pages 14–15) allowed people to listen to their own music collection wherever they were, music streaming services went a step further and offered the option to access any music anywhere.

Most devices aren't set up for 3D films, such as *Avatar*, so they have to be streamed in 2D.

Where Did It Lead?

Music streaming services such as Spotify and Apple Music, and video streaming services such as Netflix, Disney+, Amazon Prime, and YouTube were inspired by Napster. However, these services buy the rights to stream content. They earn money through paid subscriptions or ads on freemium accounts, and pay royalties to the content creators.

GENIUS

Shawn Fanning (1980–) was the developer of the software for Napster and co-founder of Napster, along with Sean Parker, who went on to be the first president of Facebook. At the time, Fanning was just 18 years old. He still works as a computer programmer and entrepreneur today.

Shawn Fanning (left) and his lawyer leaving the courtroom in 2001 after the Napster trial. Fanning managed to escape legal consequences, such as paying a fine or going to jail.

THINK BIG!

Find out about the different ways to listen to music online. How do different services and apps make money to support themselves and to pay record companies and artists? Research different approaches, such as paid subscriptions and ads. Which do you think is the most successful?

Candy Crush Saga

Following its launch in 2012, Candy Crush Saga became hugely successful as one of the first freemium games on smartphones and tablets.

The Big Idea

Candy Crush Saga is a very simple, short game, in which players win points by matching three of the same type of sweet to make them disappear. Its availability as an app on smartphones and tablets meant that it was easy to play outside of the home in spare moments. Many people quickly became fans. By 2014, 93 million people were playing a combined total of over 1 billion Candy Crush Saga games every day.

At the height of its popularity, many people played Candy Crush Saga on public transportation on the way to work or school.

How Did It Work?

Candy Crush Saga is free to download and play on a basic level, but players can pay a small fee for premium content that makes the game easier or more exciting. These microtransactions added up and, by 2013, it was estimated that King, the makers of Candy Crush Saga, earned $1 million per day through in-app purchases.

There are many microtransactions in Candy Crush Saga that offer more lives or special tools for a low price.

Where Did It Lead?

Other freemium games, such as Fortnite and Pokémon Go, have enjoyed similar success to Candy Crush Saga. However, some people criticize their use of microtransactions, stating that they often end up costing more than buying a game outright, and aren't suitable for young players, who don't understand that they are paying real money. In competitive freemium games, players who spend more money have an advantage over those who play with the basic features.

Pokémon Go combined new video and GPS technology to allow players to find and catch Pokémon in the real world.

GENIUS

Swedish game developer Sebastian Knutsson is the co-founder of King. His idea for Candy Crush Saga was to create the best "match three" game ever. He chose to base the game on candy as it is something that everyone likes!

THINK BIG!

Design your own freemium game. What content will you offer for free to attract players? Which premium features will you include to encourage players to spend money?

Oculus Rift

Oculus Rift is the first mainstream virtual reality headset. It allows gamers to get "inside" the game for an incredible gaming experience. However, the technology in the headset has the potential to go beyond entertainment into many other areas.

The Big Idea

Until recently, computer graphics were not good enough to simulate reality. The equipment needed was also too big and expensive for home gamers to use. So when Palmer Luckey presented his prototype for Oculus Rift in 2010, many people were interested and invested in a crowdfunding project to bring it to market. The first Oculus Rift headset was released in 2016.

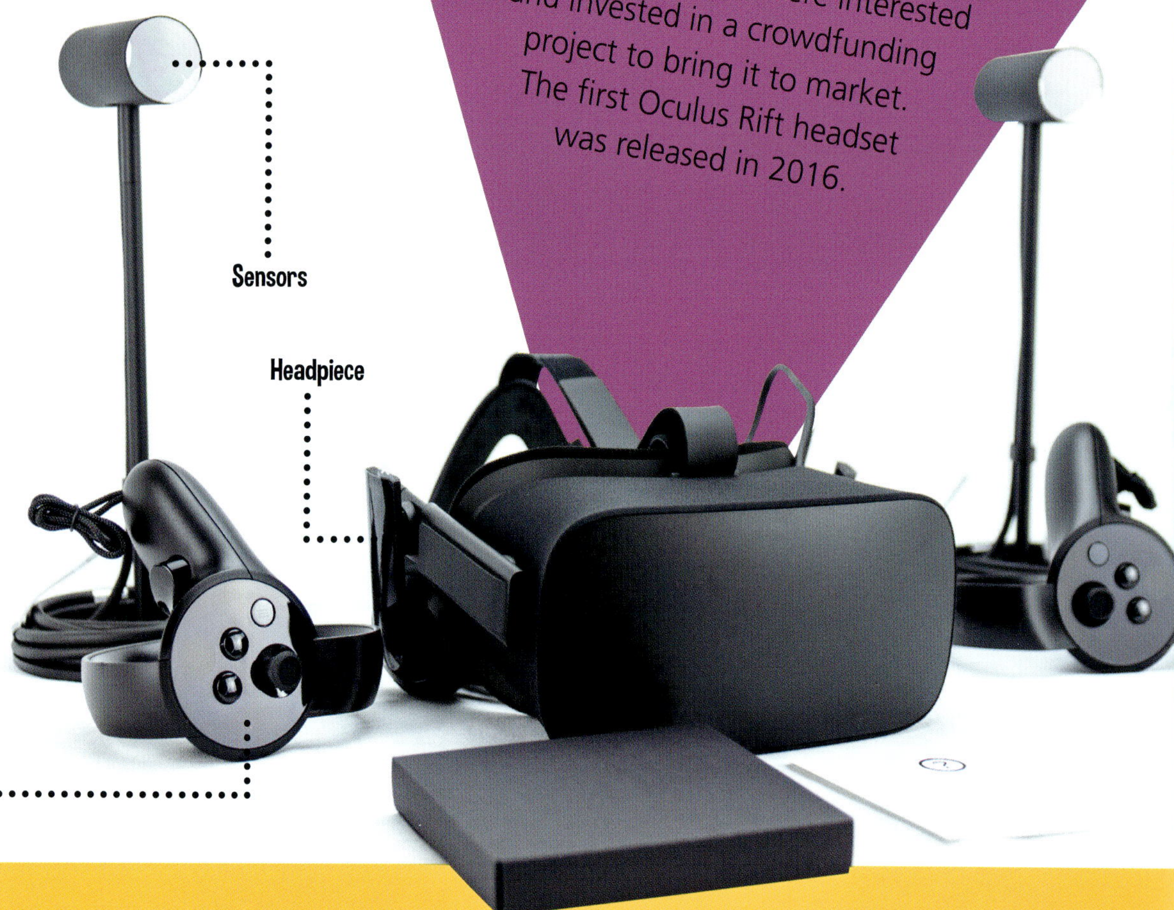

How Does It Work?

The Oculus Rift headpiece contains a screen in front of the eyes that shows incredibly realistic computer-generated images. The headpiece is connected to sensors and controllers that measure the force, direction, and position of the body. This data is sent to the headpiece, which integrates your movements into the computer-generated images to make you feel as if you are "inside" the game.

Where Did It Lead?

Virtual reality headsets offer training opportunities for situations that are often too dangerous or difficult to carry out in real life, including in space and war zones. Architects are starting to use them to offer 3D views of buildings that are yet to be built. Some people have also suggested using them to explore places that are being damaged by too much human contact, such as historic buildings or wild habitats.

Businesses can use Oculus Rift headsets to get a closer look at new products.

GENIUS

Palmer Luckey (1992–) is an American entrepreneur and inventor. He designed the first Oculus Rift prototype at the age of 18. He was very interested in electronics as a child and teenager and built his designs in his parents' garage. He went on to start Oculus VR – the company that produces the Oculus Rift.

THINK BIG!

Design a virtual reality experience. What would you like to explore using virtual reality? Why would virtual reality be a good way to do this? Make a poster advertising your experience.

Glossary

activist someone who believes strongly in social change and takes part in protests to try to make it happen

anagram a word made by using the letters from another word in a different order

animator someone who makes animated films or TV shows

bandwidth the amount of information that can be sent between computers

broadband a fast internet connection that doesn't use telephone lines

crowdfunding when lots of people each provide small amounts of money to finance a project

dial-up a slow internet connection that uses telephone lines

entrepreneur someone who starts their own business

famine when there isn't enough food for everyone in a particular country or region

freemium describes something that is free to download and use on a basic level, but requires payment for special features

grossing the highest-grossing film is the film that earned the most money before tax was taken away

interlocking firmly joined because of parts that fit together

microtransaction paying small amounts of money for special features in online games

pioneer one of the first people to do something

portable light and small enough to be carried around easily

prequel a film, book, or TV show that develops the story of another film etc by telling you what happened before that

prism a transparent piece of glass or plastic that splits light into different colors

prototype the first example of something from which later versions are developed

royalties payments made to someone who created something every time their creation is bought or used

sequel a film, book, or TV show that develops the story of another film etc by telling you what happened after that

spin-off a secondary product developed from an original, main product

streaming watching video or listening to audio directly from the internet

subscription paying money regularly to receive a service

trilogy a series of three films or books written about the same situation

virtual reality a set of images and sounds, produced by a computer, that represent a place or situation that someone can take part in

Further Information

Books

20 Fun Facts About the Internet by Kristen Rajczak Nelson (Gareth Stevens Publishing, 2024)

Walt Disney by Stephen Krensky (Crabtree Publishing, 2025)

Triumphs of Technology (STEM-gineers) by Rob Colson (Wayland, 2018)

Websites

www.lego.com/en-gb/aboutus/lego-group/the-lego-group-history

Find out more about the history of LEGO.

www.youtube.com/channel/UCUAVzSGkkTa-IoMx_x1XK4Q

Watch performances from the 1985 Live Aid concerts.

www.wizardingworld.com

Discover more about the wizarding world of Harry Potter.

Index